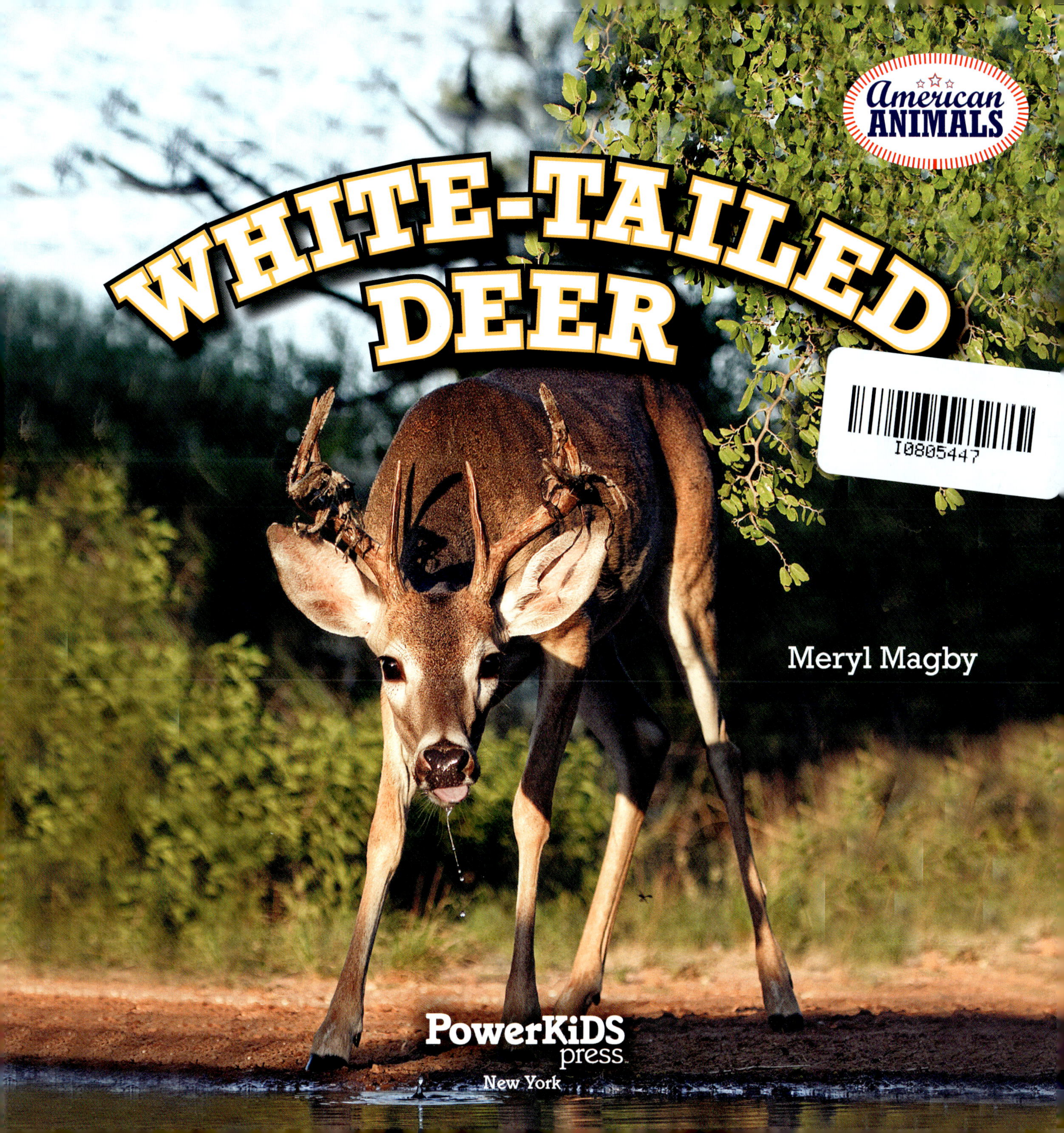

American Animals

White-Tailed Deer

Meryl Magby

PowerKiDS press
New York

Published in 2014 by The Rosen Publishing Group, Inc.
29 East 21st Street, New York, NY 10010

First Edition

Editor: Amelie von Zumbusch
Book Design: Ashley Drago
Layout Design: Colleen Bialecki

Photo Credits: Cover, p. 1 Danita Delimont/Gallo Images/Getty Images; pp. 4, 14 Tom Brakefield/Stockbyte/Thinkstock; p. 5 Ron Rowan Photography/Shutterstock.com; pp. 6–7 James Pierce/Shutterstock.com; p. 8 Bruce MacQueen/Shutterstock.com; pp. 9 (top), 15, 19 (top), 19 (bottom) iStockphoto/Thinkstock; p. 9 (bottom) Comstock/Thinkstock; pp. 10–11 Paul E. Tessler/Photodisc/Getty Images; pp. 12–13 Don Johnston/Age Photostock/Getty Images; p. 16 Dom1530/Shutterstock.com; p. 17 Debra Millet/Shutterstock.com; p. 18 Daniel J. Cox/Oxford Scientific/Getty Images; p. 20 Henry Francois Farny/The Bridgeman Art Library/Getty Images; p. 21 Hemera/Thinkstock; p. 22 Critterbiz/Shutterstock.com.

Library of Congress Cataloging-in-Publication Data

Magby, Meryl.
White-tailed deer / by Meryl Magby — First edition.
pages cm. — (American animals)
Includes index.
ISBN 978-1-4777-0792-0 (library binding) — ISBN 978-1-4777-0956-6 (pbk.) —
ISBN 978-1-4777-0957-3 (6-pack)
1. White-tailed deer—Juvenile literature. I. Title.
QL737.U55M275 2014
599.65'2–dc23

2013000750

Manufactured in the United States of America

CPSIA Compliance Information: Batch #S13PK6: For Further Information contact Rosen Publishing, New York, New York at 1-800-237-9932

Contents

Meet the White-Tailed Deer

White-tailed deer are **native** to North America. They are named for the white fur on the undersides of their tails. When a white-tailed deer gets scared, it raises its tail so the white part can be seen. White-tailed deer are known for their speed. They can run faster than 40 miles per hour (64 km/h)! This helps them get away from **predators**.

White-tailed deer are big. Despite this, they are the smallest members of the deer family in North America!

Here you can see the white underside of a white-tailed deer's tail.

White-tailed deer are the smallest deer in North America. They are closely **related** to mule deer, which are also called black-tailed deer. They are also related to other members of the deer family. These include the elk, moose, and caribou.

Fields and Forests

White-tailed deer are very common in North America. In the United States, they are found almost everywhere except for Alaska, Hawaii, and parts of the Southwest. They are also found throughout Mexico, in southern Canada, and in parts of South America.

This white-tailed deer is in a forest in Indiana. White-tailed deer live in many kinds of forests across North America.

White-tailed deer live in many **habitats**. Their favorite places to live are shady forests near green fields and meadows. However, they also make their homes in farmlands, dry deserts, and wet swamps with tall grass. White-tailed deer habitats need to have plants for the deer to eat and water for them to drink. The deer also need places to rest and hide from predators.

Long Legs and Strong Noses

White-tailed deer stand about 3 feet (1 m) tall at the shoulder. They have long legs and **hooved** feet. This lets them run fast and jump high. Their large ears **rotate** to help them hear sounds in all directions. Their powerful noses can pick up smells 100 times better than human noses can!

In summer, white-tailed deer are reddish-brown or tan. Their throats, their stomachs, and the undersides of their tails are white. In winter, their coats fade to grayish-brown.

White-tailed deer have black noses. They generally have small patches of white around their eyes and noses.

Adult male deer are called bucks. Bucks grow a pair of antlers each spring. The antlers are made of bone. In winter, bucks shed their antlers.

The points of a buck's antlers are called tines.

A deer's summer coat is made up of short, stiff hairs.

Crashing Antlers

Adult female deer are called does. Does live in groups with other does and their babies, called fawns. These groups sometimes include more than 25 does and fawns. Bucks stay separate from does and fawns for most of the year. They live alone or in small groups of between 2 and 4 bucks.

These white-tailed bucks are fighting during the rut. The rut generally takes place in fall or early winter.

Each fall, white-tailed deer have a **mating** season. This is called the rut. During the rut, bucks fight with each other over does and **territory**. They crash their antlers together and stomp their hooves against the ground. The winners of the fights get to mate with the most does.

White-Tailed Deer Facts

1. When bucks first grow their antlers in the spring, they have a soft covering called velvet. In the fall, bucks rub their antlers against trees to help shed the velvet.

2. White-tailed deer can leap high into the air. They can easily jump over a 9-foot (3-m) fence!

3. Bucks often weigh between 150 and 300 pounds (68–136 kg). Does are smaller. They weigh between 90 and 200 pounds (41–91 kg).

4. Some people think that you can tell the age of a male deer by how many tines his antlers have. However, the size of a buck's antlers depends on the **nutrients** in his diet, not his age.

5. White-tailed deer are good swimmers. They can swim about 13 miles per hour (21 km/h).

6. About one-third of white-tailed deer in the United States live in Texas.

7. After a buck sheds his antlers, they are often eaten by small animals such as porcupines, rabbits, and rodents. This is because the antlers are a good source of calcium and other nutrients.

8. White-tailed deer have **glands** on the backs of their hooves that help them leave behind smells. They leave these smells to **communicate** with other deer.

Does and Fawns

Does give birth to fawns in the spring. Fawns are born with reddish-brown fur covered in small white spots. Their coats help them blend in with their habitats. This helps keep them safe from predators. Fawns can stand up and walk right away.

A doe may have one, two, or three fawns at a time.

The spots on this white-tailed fawn's coat help it blend in with the fallen leaves and shadows on the forest floor.

Fawns drink their mother's milk. Does hide their fawns in the forest or fields when they go look for food for themselves. The fawns lie flat on the ground so predators cannot see them. After about eight weeks, fawns look for food with their mothers. Female fawns often stay with their mothers for two years. Males often leave after one year.

Many Kinds of Plants

White-tailed deer are **herbivores**. This means they eat only plants. Depending on the season, deer may eat leaves, grass, twigs, fruits, nuts, alfalfa, lichen, or pinecones.

Which plants white-tailed deer eat depends on both the deer's habitat and the time of year.

Deer look for food in the early morning around sunrise and in the late afternoon around sunset. They follow paths called trails to feeding areas. White-tailed deer use the same trails over and over again.

Deer's teeth help them eat tough plants. They have sharp teeth for biting and flat teeth for grinding their food. Deer eat quickly. Sometimes, they cough up their food and chew it again later!

In fall, deer may look for plants growing under fallen leaves. In winter, they may have to search under the snow.

Outrunning Predators

Deer have two-toed feet with sturdy hooves. Their hooves help make deer sure-footed runners.

Wild white-tailed deer have several animal predators. Bobcats, mountain lions, wolves, coyotes, bears, and feral dogs all hunt white-tailed deer. Predators often try to catch fawns instead of adult deer. This is because fawns are smaller than adult deer and not as quick.

White-tailed deer have good eyesight and hearing. They use their noses to smell when predators are nearby, too. Deer are quick to run when they sense danger. Their long legs help them quickly leap and run through the plants and trees in thick fields and forests. Their speed helps them get away from predators.

Lynx hunt white-tailed deer fawns. However, they do not generally hunt adult deer.

Wolves hunt both adult white-tailed deer and fawns.

Deer and People

People and white-tailed deer have a long history in North America. Native American peoples have long hunted white-tailed deer. When early American settlers came from Europe, they also started to hunt deer. Deer are hunted for their meat, which is called venison. They are hunted for their skins as well. People make leather from deer's skins, which are also called hides.

This painting shows a Native American coming back from a deer hunt in the early twentieth century. Deer was a key food for many Native American peoples.

In places where there are too many of them, deer can become pests. They eat plants on farms and in people's gardens. Sometimes, they even spread diseases.

Today, white-tailed deer are a favorite big **game** for hunters in North America. They are hunted across the United States for their meat and for sport. In many places, hunters help keep deer **populations** from getting too large.

Too Many Deer

Scientists think that there might be as many as 30 million white-tailed deer in the United States!

Today, the white-tailed deer population in North America is very large. However, there are not enough deer predators, such as mountain lions and wolves. These predators have almost died out because of overhunting. When there are too many deer, there is not enough food to go around. Some deer are in danger of starving. Deer also harm forests by eating too many plants.

Wildlife groups are trying to keep deer predators and their habitats safe. More predators will help keep the deer population from getting too large!

Glossary

communicate (kuh-MYOO-nih-kayt) To share facts or feelings.

game (GAYM) Wild animals that are hunted for food.

glands (GLANDZ) Body parts that produce things that help a body run.

habitats (HA-buh-tats) The kinds of land where an animal or a plant naturally lives.

herbivores (ER-buh-vorz) Animals that eat only plants.

hooved (HOOVD) Having hard coverings on the feet.

mating (MAYT-ing) Coming together to make babies.

native (NAY-tiv) Born or grown in a certain place or country.

nutrients (NOO-tree-ents) Food that a living thing needs to live and grow.

populations (pop-yoo-LAY-shunz) Groups of animals or people living in the same place.

predators (PREH-duh-terz) Animals that kill other animals for food.

related (rih-LAYT-ed) Part of the same family.

rotate (ROH-tayt) To move in a circle.

territory (TER-uh-tor-ee) Land or space that animals guard for their use.

Index

Websites

Due to the changing nature of Internet links, PowerKids Press has developed an online list of websites related to the subject of this book. This site is updated regularly. Please use this link to access the list:
www.powerkidslinks.com/amer/deer/